The Artistry of Fundamentals *for Band*

Frank Erickson

Contents

D1275475

Copyright © MCMXCII by Alfred Publishing Co., Inc.
All rights reserved. Printed in USA.

Art Direction: Ted Engelbart
Cover Design and Illustration: Martin Ledyard
Project Editor: Dave Black

UNIT 1
Bb Major/ G Minor (Concert)

Doxology and Variation

Scale Study

Scale Harmony

In scale and arpeggio exercises that normally do not contain articulations, articulations such as the following may be applied:

G Minor (Concert)

Harmonic Minor

Chromatic Scale

Arpeggios

Intervals

Rhythm Study No. 1

The rhythms throughout this book can be played in three different ways:
1. Play all eight rhythms on one note;
2. Select one rhythm and play it on each note of the scale;
3. Play all eight rhythms, each one on a different note of the scale.

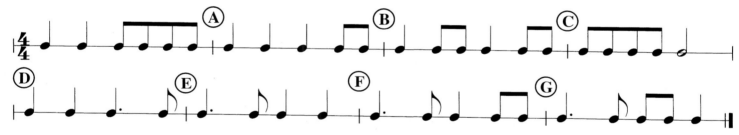

First Etude

4

Rhythm Round

G Minor (Concert) Etude

Articulations

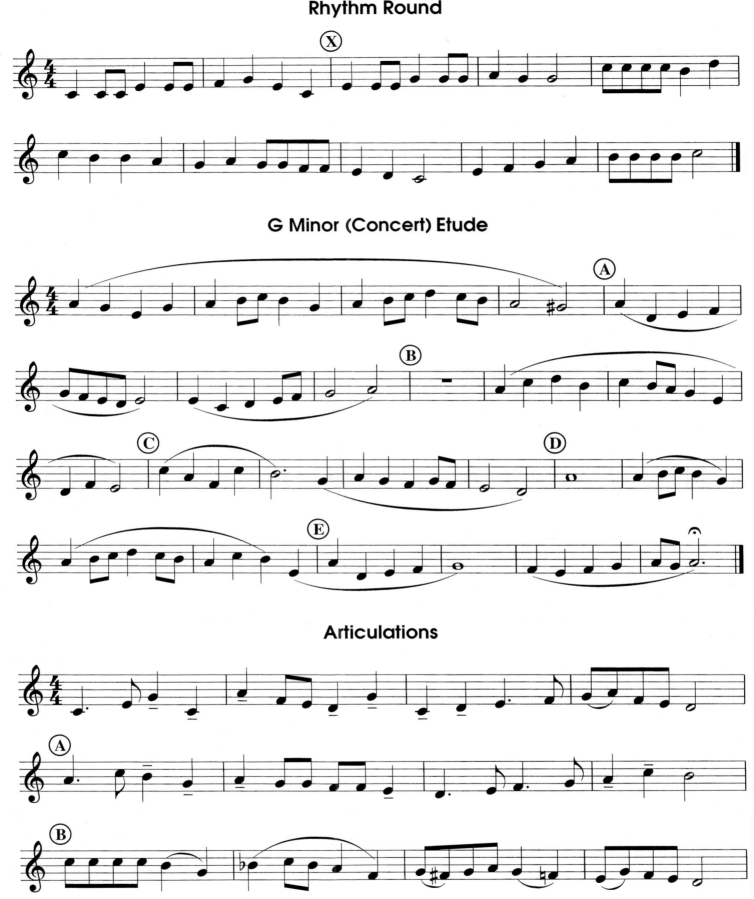

Rhythm Study No. 2

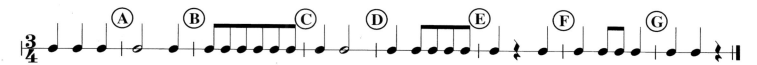

3/4 Etude

Speed Drill

Start slowly then gradually increase speed. Use the articulations that are suggested in Unit 1, Sample Articulations.

UNIT 2
F Major/ D Minor (Concert)

Chorale

Scale Study

Scale Harmony

D Minor (Concert)

Melodic Minor

Arpeggios

Intervals

Chromatic Round

Rhythm Study No. 1

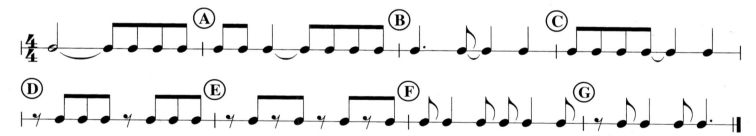

Pickups and Ties

8

After–Beat Etude

Rhythm Round

Syncopation Etude

Rhythm Study No. 2

Variation Etude

Speed Drill

UNIT 3
C Major/ A Minor (Concert)

Eternal Father, Strong to Save

Scale Study

Scale Harmony

A Minor (Concert)

Natural Minor

Chromatic Etude

Arpeggios

Intervals

Rhythm Study

Sixteenths

Dotted Eighths and Sixteenths

Rhythm Round

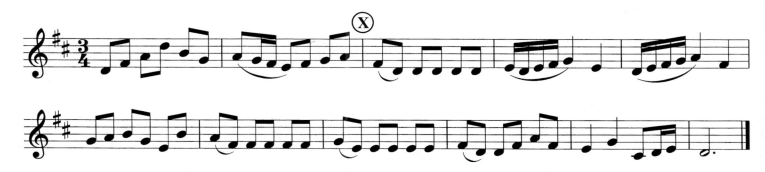

Rhythm Variations

Changing Meters No. 1

Changing Meters No. 2

Speed Drill

UNIT 4
Eb Major /C Minor (Concert)

Chorale

Arpeggios

Intervals

Chromatic Round

Rhythm Round

Rhythm Study No. 1

16

Triple Meters

6/8 Time

Rhythm Study No. 2

Alla Breve

Alla Breve Variations

Syncopation Etude

Speed Drill

UNIT 5
G Major/ E Minor (Concert)

Lo, How a Rose E'er Blooming

Scale Study

Scale Harmony

E Minor (Concert)

Melodic Minor

Arpeggios

Chromatic Etude

Intervals

Rhythm Round

Rhythm Study No. 1

5/8 Time

Rhythm Study No. 2

2/4–5/8

Sixteenths in 3/4

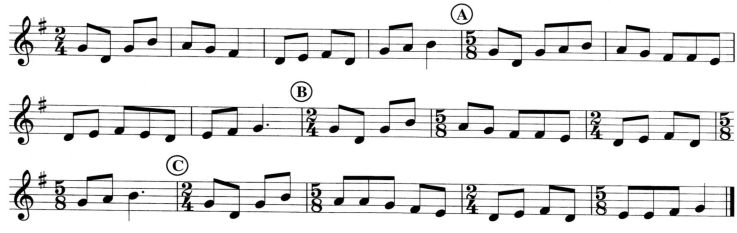

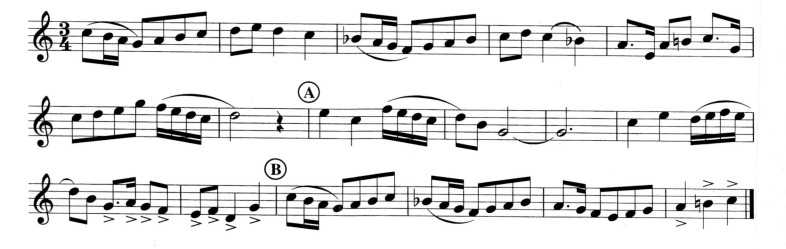

Articulations No. 1

Articulations No. 2

Speed Drill

UNIT 6
Ab Major/ F Minor(Concert)

Chaconne Chorale

Scale Study

Scale Harmony

F Minor (Concert)

Arpeggios

Intervals

Chromatic Round

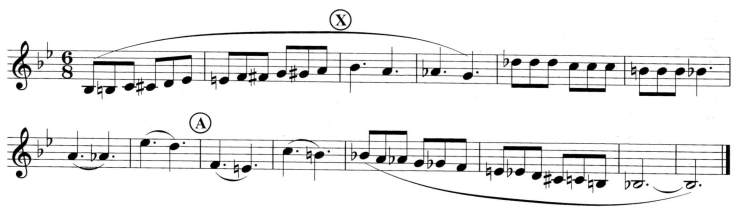

Rhythm Round

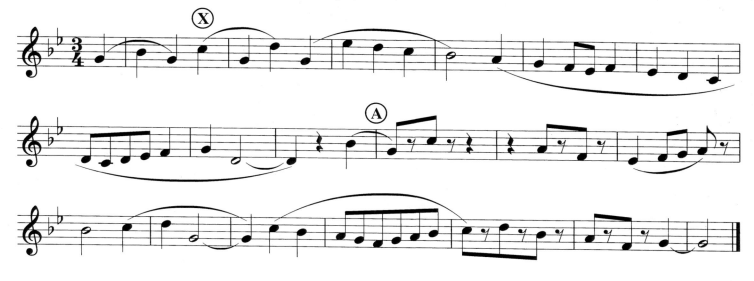

Rhythm Study

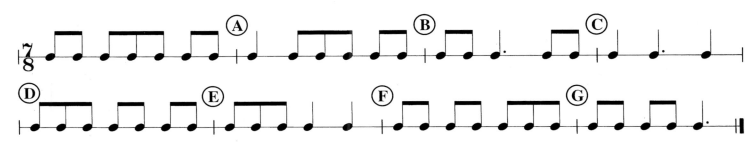

7/8 Time

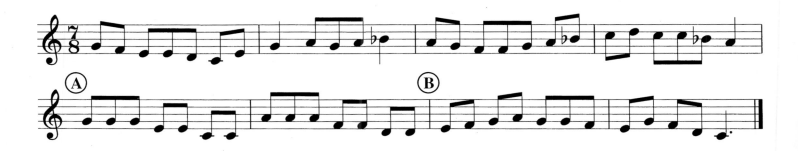

Mixed Rhythms

F Minor (Concert) Etude

Staccato-Rest Etude

Duplets and Triplets

Speed Drill

UNIT 7
Db Major/ Bb Minor(Concert)

Piae Cationes

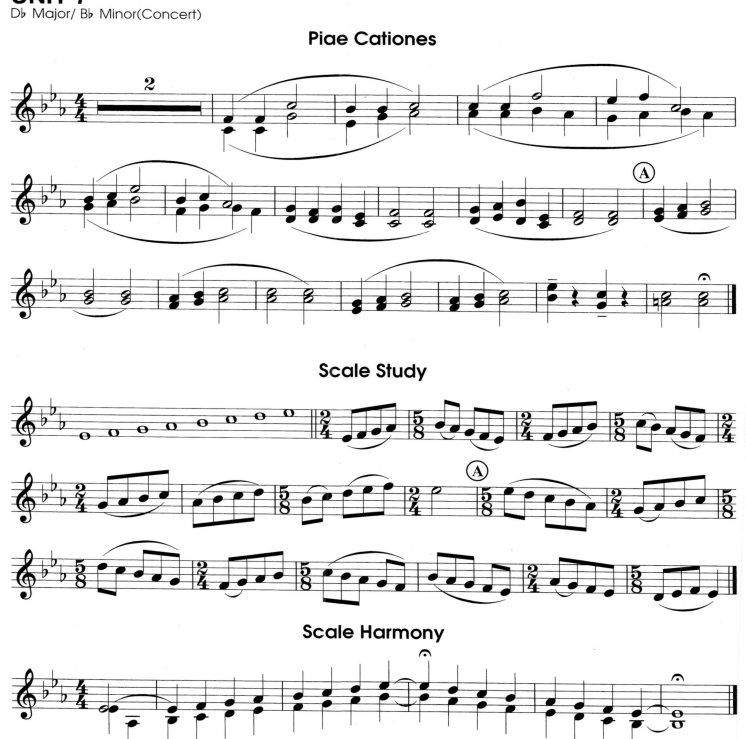

Scale Study

Scale Harmony

Bb Minor (Concert)

Harmonic Minor

Arpeggios

Intervals

Chromatic Etude

Rhythm Round

Quarter–Note Triplets

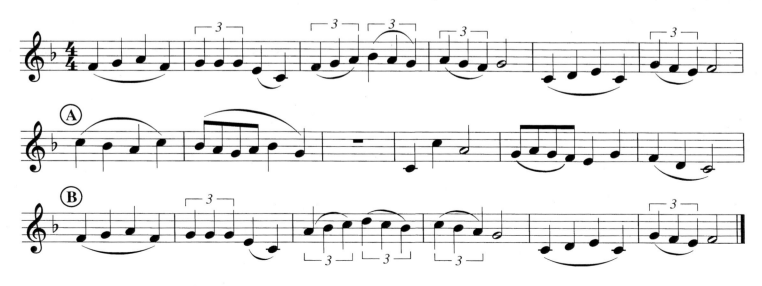

Rhythm Study No. 1

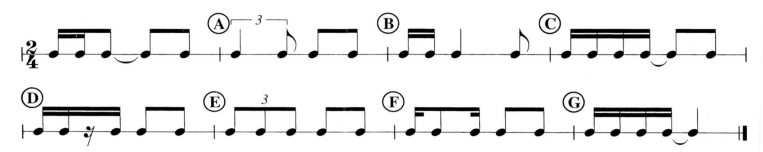

Syncopation Etude

More Sixteenths

Rhythm Study No. 2

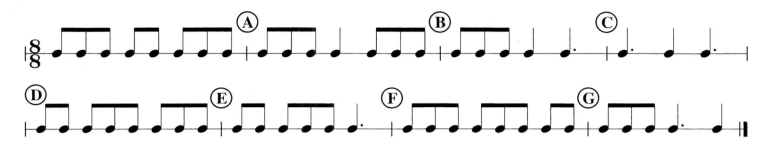

8/8 Time

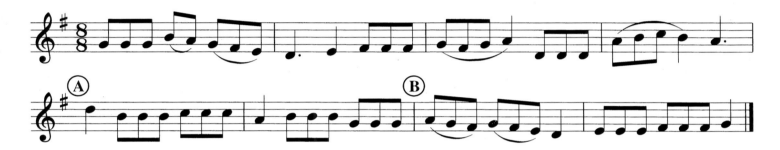

Forte–Piano

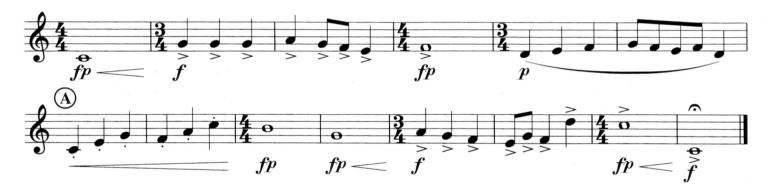

Speed Drill

UNIT 8
D Major/B Minor (Concert)

Passacaglia Chorale

Scale Study

Scale Harmony

B Minor (Concert)

Melodic Minor

Arpeggios

Chromatic Intervals

Rhythm Round

Variations

Rhythm Study No.1

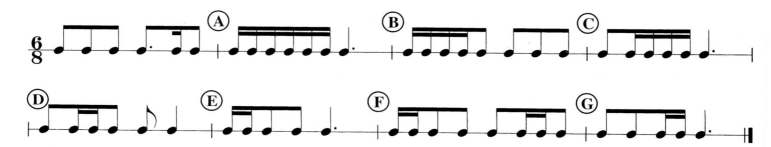

6/8 Challenge

Dotted Eighth and Sixteenth Pickups

Rhythm Study No.2

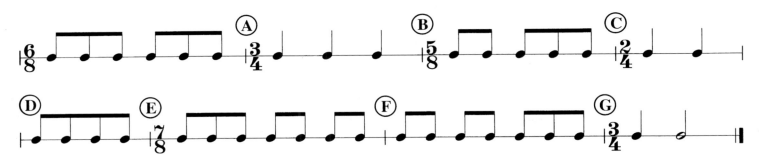

Changing Meters

Speed Drill

APPENDIX

Major Scales

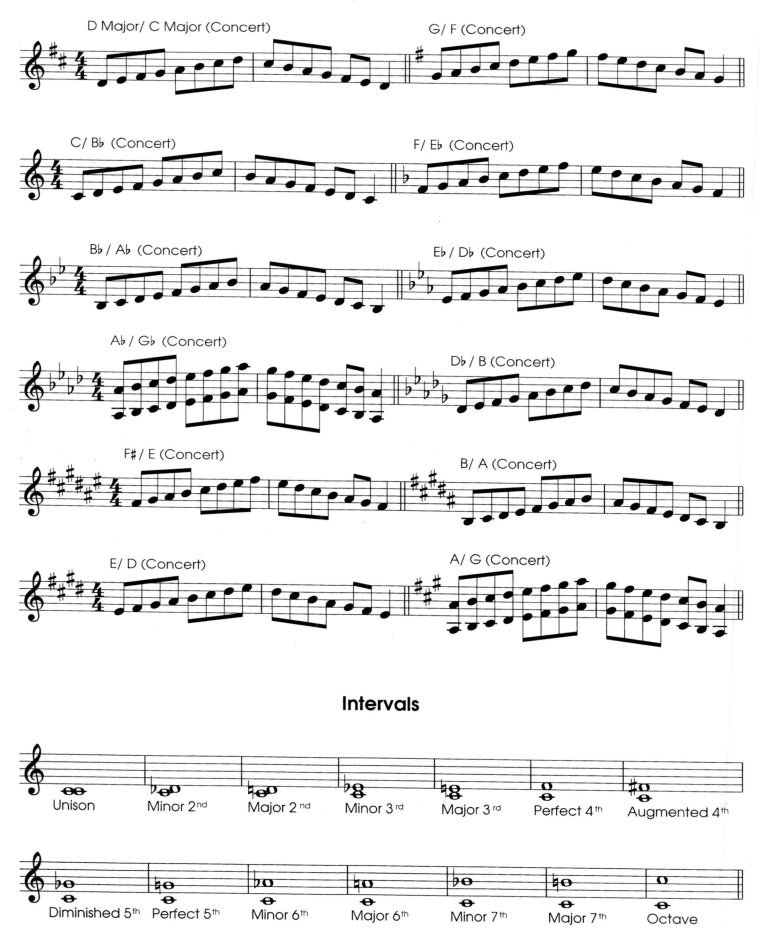

Intervals

Lip Slurs for Brass No.1

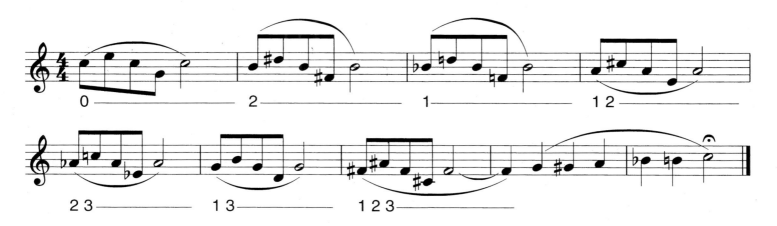

Lip Slurs for Brass No.2

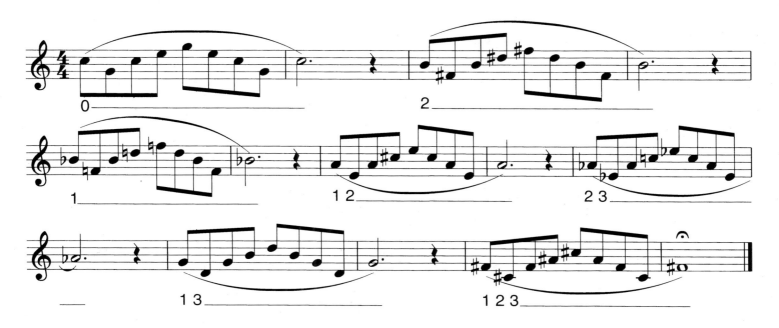

Chords

M – Major   + – Augmented
m – minor   o – Diminished

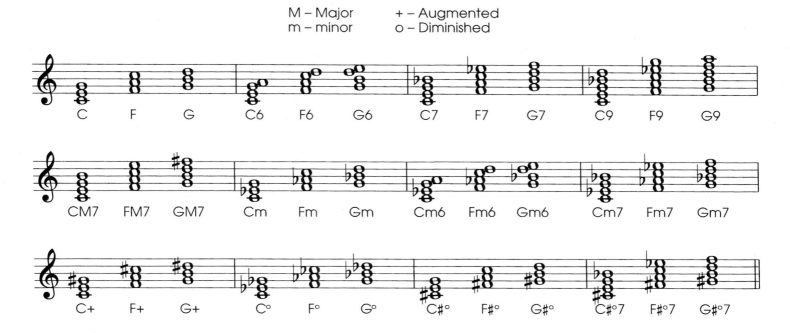

Rhythms with Rests